6539125

£29.99 F

Enhancing   I R

Vulbe

of related interest

Helping Adolescents and Adults to Build Self-Esteem
A Photocopiable Resource Book
Deborah Plummer
ISBN 1 84310 185 8

Helping Children to Build Self-Esteem
A Photocopiable Activities Book
Deborah Plummer
ISBN 1 85302 927 0

**Assessing and Developing Communication and Thinking Skills
in People with Autism and Communication Difficulties**
A Toolkit for Parents and Professionals
Kate Silver, Autism Initiatives
ISBN 1 84310 352 4

**Social Skills Training for Adolescents with General Moderate
Learning Difficulties**
Ursula Cornish and Fiona Ross
ISBN 1 84310 179 3

People Skills for Young Adults
Márianna Csóti
ISBN 1 85302 716 2

**Relationship Development Intervention with Children,
Adolescents and Adults**
Social and Emotional Development Activities for Asperger Syndrome,
Autism, PDD and NLD
Steven E. Gutstein and Rachelle K. Sheely
ISBN 1 84310 717 1

Enhancing Self-Esteem

A Self-Esteem Training Package for Individuals with Disabilities

**Nick Hagiliassis and
Hrepsime Gulbenkoglu**

**Jessica Kingsley Publishers
London and Philadelphia**

First published in 2002 by Scope (Vic.) Ltd.

This edition published in 2005
by Jessica Kingsley Publishers
116 Pentonville Road
London N1 9JB, UK
and
400 Market Street, Suite 400
Philadelphia, PA 19106, USA

www.jkp.com

Library of Congress Cataloging in Publication Data
A CIP catalog record for this book is available from the Library of Congress

British Library Cataloguing in Publication Data
A CIP catalogue record for this book is available from the British Library

ISBN-10: 1 84310 353 2
ISBN-13: 978 1 84310 353 0

Printed and Bound in Great Britain by
Athenaeum Press, Gateshead, Tyne and Wear

This training package provides a starting point for the development of self-esteem in individuals with physical and multiple disabilities. While all care has been taken in the preparation of the training package, in no event shall the authors, the various collaborators, Jessica Kingsley Publishers, or Scope (Vic.) Ltd. be liable for any damages or consequences resulting from direct, indirect, correct or incorrect use of this training package. It is the responsibility of the user to ensure that the training package is appropriate for the individual. This training package should *not* be used as a substitute for seeking professional diagnosis, treatment and care.

Contents

List of Hand-outs

Acknowledgements

The authors would like to greatly acknowledge all those individuals who contributed to the development of this training package. In particular, we would like to thank the clients who over the years have shared with us their experiences and insights, on which a significant portion of this package is based. We would also like to thank Denise West and Helen Larkin for their support and encouragement, our colleagues for their ideas and input, and Scope (Vic.) Ltd. management for providing us with the opportunity to develop this package.

Introduction

Positive self-esteem is the capacity to view oneself with a sense of value and competence. It is the inner belief that we can meet the challenges of our existence.

(Frank and Edwards 1988, p.1)

Healthy self-esteem is widely viewed as critical to psychological well-being and is thought to underlie feelings of adequacy, strength and self-confidence. Individuals with healthy self-esteem are likely to be better at working on and achieving their goals, dealing with and adjusting to new situations, handling challenges and frustrations, and asserting themselves. They are more likely to have a better sense of control over their own lives and a greater sense of empowerment. The virtues of healthy self-esteem are obvious and are highlighted by a number of authors (e.g. Canfield and Wells 1976; Kriegsman, Zaslow and D'Zmura-Rechsteiner 1992; Tonks 1990).

While healthy self-esteem is important to us all, it is an issue that appears particularly relevant to people with disabilities. This is because people with disabilities may be faced with a unique range of challenges associated with having a disability, such as negative messages, low expectations, reduced opportunities and outright discrimination (Frank and Edwards 1988). Just how well an individual contends with these challenges and the impact of these challenges on their psychological well-being, will depend very much on the strength of their self-esteem. For this reason, supporting people with disabilities to explore and enhance their self-esteem is a high priority.

About the package

The package is designed for adults with physical and multiple disabilities and will be most suitable for people with a mild intellectual disability and/or severe communication impairment. The development of the package was motivated by a need, perceived by the authors, for more specialised resource materials in this area for this group. Specifically, it was felt the self-esteem needs of many adults with disabilities could be better met through the availability of a comprehensive resource with content that is relevant, cognitively suitable and age-appropriate.

Additionally, it was felt important to make such a programme accessible to individuals with severe communication impairment. The package has been developed to meet these needs.

The package is intended as a starting point for the enhancement of specific self-esteem related skills. The skills covered in the package are based on the experiences of the authors and information from the relevant literature. They comprise skills related to exploration of individuality, emotional awareness, thought awareness, body image and acceptance of self, assertiveness, social skills, problem solving and nurturing success.

Ten sessions have been constructed covering these skills:

1.   What is self-esteem?
2.   What makes us special?
3.   Feeling good.
4.   Healthy thinking.
5.   Accepting who we are.
6.   Speaking up for ourselves.
7.   Communicating well.
8.   Handling problems.
9.   Reaching our goals.
10. Putting it all together.

Each session is intended to last for two hours, including a fifteen-minute break; however, some timing variations may occur from session to session as determined by the needs of the group. Sessions are fully scripted, and detailed instructions are given on how to run each session. However, it is important to emphasise that while a script is provided, given the nature of this type of group, it may not always be possible to adhere rigidly to the scripts. Each session is effectively a self-contained unit. It is vital that the sessions are delivered in the sequence in which they appear in the package, and that all sessions are presented.

Each session follows a specific format and includes a list of the materials required each week, activities, hand-outs and reviews of what has already been learnt. Facilitators may find it helpful to go through the materials required before each session, identifying which hand-outs need to be photocopied, which (if any) need cutting out, and whether the participants need to be asked to bring anything to the session. All materials needed are provided in the photocopiable hand-outs following the activities. For a couple of activities the facilitator or participants need to bring something extra, such as a 'same and different objects' bag for Activity 2.1 or a photo of themselves for Activity 5.4. The hand-outs have a strong emphasis on pictographic symbols. This is to support individuals in their understanding of the information presented. In addition, it is recommended that for individuals with severe communication impairment, facilitators utilise established communication systems (e.g. electronic communication aids) and other communication methods (e.g. gestures, signs). It is important to acknowledge that even with the use of pictographs, some individuals may still exhibit comprehension difficulties. Individuals in this circumstance may require content modifications or more individualised support.

The sessions are developed in accordance with basic learning principles. Active learning is emphasised in that participants are actively encouraged to be involved in sessions rather than being passive observers. Role-play is used with the aim of giving participants opportunities to practise behaviours in hypothetical situations that can then be generalised to real-life situations. Repetition is also used to reinforce the learning of concepts and skills.

Clearly, the facilitator will have a key role in relation to the delivery of the package material, timing of sessions and any adjustments to the content of the session. At a more general level, the facilitator will need to have effective group leadership skills and have a strong grounding in group dynamics. The facilitator will also need to be responsive to the needs of individuals with learning difficulties or severe communication impairment. The package requires that the facilitator have prior and extensive knowledge of cognitive behaviour techniques.

The package is designed for use with a maximum of ten participants and it is recommended that these individuals have a similar level of abilities. Note that sessions afford an important role to the participants' support people in terms of enabling the participants to be maximally involved in the sessions, and ensuring there is appropriate follow-up of session aims.

Session 1

What is Self-Esteem?

Aims of this session

1.   Introduce participants to each other.

2.   Have participants get to know each other a little better.

3.   Present rules of group work.

4.   Introduce concept of self and self-esteem.

5.   Conduct a brief assessment of self-esteem.

6.   Present an overview of material to be covered in sessions.

Materials required

- 'Getting to know you' sheets.

- 'My self-esteem' sheets.

Session plan

Introduce participants to each other

- Introduce facilitator/s.

- Welcome group participants.

- Present a brief overview of purpose of group – to further develop our self-esteem (emphasise that we will discuss what 'self-esteem' means).

- Have each member and their support person introduce themselves.

- Discuss 'housekeeping' issues (for example, time of group, location of group, location of amenities).

Have participants get to know each other a little better

Emphasise that, before beginning to discuss self-esteem, it is important that we get to know each other a little better.

ACTIVITY 1.1

Participants form groups of two (preferably with someone they are unfamiliar with). Participants then interview each other using the 'Getting to know you' sheets, and fill in the answers in the space provided, with assistance if required. At the completion of the interviews, the facilitator asks participants to report back their interview information.

For example, Brian has got to know Mary.
'Brian, who did you get to know?'
'Where does Mary live?'

Getting to know you (1)

 **What is your name?**

_____

 **Who did you get to know?**

_____

 **Where does this person live?**

_____

Getting to know you (2)

What does this person like to do?

_____

What is this person's least favourite food?

_____

What does this person do during the week?

_____

Review 1.1

Up until now, we have:

- got to know each other a little better. This is to help us feel more comfortable with each other.

Present rules of group work

Now we will discuss some of the rules of group work.

Ask if any participants have been involved in group work before and about their experiences of this. Emphasise that in order for the group to run fairly and be successful for everyone, it is important to:

- let one person communicate at a time

- listen to others when they are communicating

- respect each other's thoughts and feelings, even though they may be different from ours

- let everyone have a go and share the conversation around

- only say what we feel comfortable saying

- respect each other's privacy.

Review 1.2

Up until now, we have:

- got to know each other a little better

- talked about some of the rules of working in a group. This is to help the group run well.

Introduce the concept of self and self-esteem

Now, we will begin to discuss self-esteem.

Ask participants what they think is meant by self. Emphasise that your self is you.

Your self-esteem is how you feel about you. Some people feel good about themselves (they like themselves). These people are said to have high self-esteem. Some people feel bad about themselves (they do not like themselves). These people are said to have low self-esteem.

It is very important to feel good about yourself and to like yourself. It's good to have high self-esteem. Ask participants why they think it is important to have high self-esteem. Emphasise that people with high self-esteem are:

- better at reaching their goals (with high self-esteem, you are much more likely to work towards your goals, or at least have a go)

- better at handling problems (with high self-esteem, you are better able to deal with problems in your day-to-day life)

- better at coping with disappointments (with high self-esteem, you are much more likely to 'bounce back' from disappointments)

- better at handling criticism (with high self-esteem, you are much more likely to take criticisms 'on the chin')

- better at speaking up for themselves (with high self-esteem, you are much more likely to let others know what you really want and what your true feelings are)

- better able to adjust to change (with high self-esteem, you are much more likely to accept new ideas and ways of doing things).

In general, if you feel good about yourself, if you like yourself and if you have high self-esteem, you are much better off. That is why it is important that we start to think about our self-esteem, and try to help our self-esteem develop further.

Ask participants why they think it is that some people have high self-esteem, while others have low self-esteem. Emphasise that our self-esteem usually depends on the sorts of experiences we have had through our lives (for example, experiences with family, friends, staff, people in the community and others). People with high self-esteem have usually had lots of nice experiences in their lives. People with low self-esteem have usually had many unpleasant experiences in their lives. But no single experience can determine your self-esteem.

Review 1.3

Up until now, we have:

- got to know each other a little better

- talked about some of the rules of working in a group

- talked about high self-esteem and low self-esteem. We said that it's good to have high self-esteem.

Conduct a brief assessment of self-esteem

Let's look at our own self-esteem.

ACTIVITY 1.2

For this activity, participants complete a brief self-esteem assessment using the 'My self-esteem' sheets. The facilitator reads each statement aloud, and participants indicate on their sheets, by ticking 'Yes' or 'No', whether the statement applies to them. Participants then add up their responses (each 'Yes' response is given a score of one) and enter their total score in the appropriate section. Emphasise that most people feel bad about themselves from time to time, so when answering the questions, participants should think about how they feel most of the time.

The actual scores are not disclosed to the group. Rather, the general implication of low and high scores is discussed. For low scores, this means that participants' self-esteem could probably be developed further. For high scores, this means that participants' self-esteem is probably healthy overall, but may still need some work in specific areas (that is, in the areas where they have responded 'No').

✓

My self-esteem (1)

I am a good person ☐ Yes ☐ No

**I let people
know how I feel** ☐ Yes ☐ No

I think calmly ☐ Yes ☐ No

I like the way I look ☐ Yes ☐ No

I focus on my abilities ☐ Yes ☐ No

My self-esteem (2)

I am proud of the things I've done ☐ Yes ☐ No

I set goals ☐ Yes ☐ No

I can stand up for myself ☐ Yes ☐ No

I communicate well with others ☐ Yes ☐ No

TOTAL SCORE _____

Review 1.4

Up until now, we have:

- got to know each other a little better

- talked about some of the rules of working in a group

- talked about high self-esteem and low self-esteem

- learned a bit more about our own self-esteem to see what areas we can improve upon.

Present an overview of material to be covered in sessions

Emphasise that self-esteem is something that is always changing, and something that we can improve. This group aims to help each participant improve their self-esteem. To achieve this, we will learn more about different parts of our selves.

The areas we will be looking at over the next number of weeks are:

- what makes us special?

- feeling good

- healthy thinking

- accepting who we are

- speaking up for ourselves

- communicating well

- handling problems

- reaching our goals

- putting it all together.

To help us learn about these areas, we will talk about them and use activities. We will also set goals that are important for you to follow up on when you finish the sessions (with help from your support person if needed).

Summary of Session 1

Today we:

- got to know each other a little better

- talked about some of the rules of working in a group

- talked about high self-esteem and low self-esteem

- learned a bit more about our own self-esteem

- talked about what we are going to learn about over our sessions.

Session 2

What Makes Us Special?

Aims of this session

1. Briefly review summary points from the last session.

2. Highlight that people are both the same as and different from others.

3. Explore in what ways people can be different from each other.

4. Highlight that doing things in different ways is OK.

5. Explore the link between a sense of uniqueness and self-esteem.

Materials required

- 'Same and different' bag of objects (to be organised by the facilitator).

- 'Getting around' and 'Communicating' cards.

- 'Someone I admire' sheets.

- 'What makes me special?' sheets.

Session plan

Briefly review summary points from the last session

Facilitators should review the summary points from the last session.

Highlight that people are both the same as and different from others

Ask participants what they think is meant by 'same' and what is meant by 'different'. Emphasise that 'same' is when two things have something in common or are alike (for example, two people can have the same colour hair). 'Different' is when two things have something that makes them special or unique (for example, two people can have different coloured eyes). Often, two things can be both the same as, but also different from, each other.

ACTIVITY 2.1

For this activity, each participant is asked to select two objects from a bag provided and organised by the facilitator. The bag should contain a range of similar objects (for example, a big blue plate, a small blue plate, a blunt blue pencil, a short blue pencil, a long blue pencil). Each participant states one thing that is the same about the items selected, and one thing that is different about the items.

For example, a participant pulls out of the bag a big blue plate and a long blue pencil. They may say, 'One thing that is the same is that they are both blue; one thing that is different is you eat off one, and draw with the other.'

Now, participants are asked to identify one thing that is the same about themselves and the person sitting next to them, for example, 'We both have blue eyes.'

Next, participants are asked to identify one thing that is different between themselves and the same person sitting next to them, for example, 'She has brown hair and I have blonde hair.'

Emphasise that we can be the same as and also different from others.

> **Review 2.1**
>
> Up until now we have:
>
> - talked about same and different. This is to help us understand that we are the same as, and also different from, others.

Explore in what ways people can be different from each other

Emphasise that each of us is different in many ways. Ask participants if they can identify some of the ways we can be different to others.

Examples include:

- the way we look
- the way we think
- the way we feel
- our likes and dislikes
- the sorts of attitudes we have
- the sorts of experiences we have had
- the types of families and friends we have
- the places we work and live
- and so on…

ACTIVITY 2.2

For this activity, the facilitator asks participants questions to generate group discussion around different preferences.

Questions:

'What is your favourite TV show?'

'Which football team do you support?'

'What do you like to do in your free time?'

Emphasise that there are many ways in which people can be different from each other, such as in their likes and dislikes.

Review 2.2

Up until now we have:

- talked about same and different

- said that there are many ways in which people can be different from each other. This is to help us to understand that many differences can exist between people.

Highlight that doing things in different ways is OK

Emphasise that there are many ways we can do things differently from others.

ACTIVITY 2.3

For this activity, the 'Getting around' and 'Communicating' cards are used. Participants are presented with the cards and are prompted to identify the general task represented, then the different ways that task is being achieved. Facilitators may need to obscure the card headings ('Getting around' and 'Communicating') so as not to give away the answers when showing the cards to participants.

Card	General task being represented	Different ways task is being achieved
'Getting around'	Getting around	• Independent walking • Electric wheelchair • Manual wheelchair
'Communicating'	Communication	• Speech • Communication board • Electronic aid

Emphasise that there are many ways we can do things. For each task, what is important is that we achieve our goal. How we do it is less important. For example, in the 'Getting around' card we have three people getting around. One person is walking independently, another is using a manual wheelchair, while another is using a motorised wheelchair. They are all getting around; they are all going to places they want to go. But each is doing this in a different way. Each of these ways is OK.

Likewise, on the 'communicating card', we have three people communicating. One person is using their voice, another person is using a communication board, while the third person is using an electronic aid. They are all communicating and they are all getting their message across. But each is doing this in a different way. Each of these ways is OK.

Getting around card

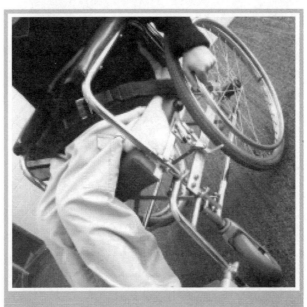

Manual wheelchair

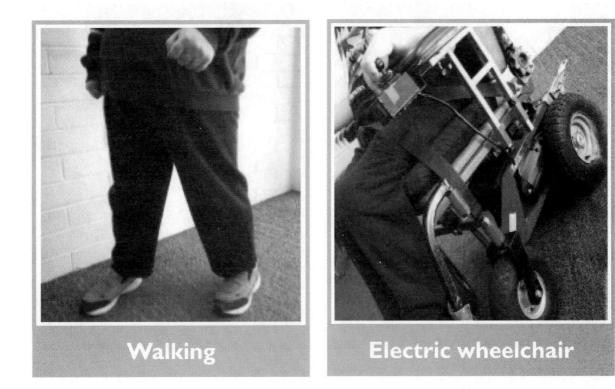

Walking

Electric wheelchair

Communicating card

Communication board

Speech

Electronic aid

Review 2.3

Up until now we have:

- talked about same and different

- said that there are many ways in which people can be different from each other

- seen that people can do things differently. It is OK to do things differently from others.

Explore the link between a sense of uniqueness and self-esteem

Emphasise that when we acknowledge our differences, we also acknowledge our individuality. Our differences are what make us special.

ACTIVITY 2.4

Participants are given the 'Someone I admire' sheets and are asked to think of one person that they admire (such as a family member, a famous person or a friend), and to think of one thing that makes this person different or unique. Participants then present their responses to the group. Emphasise that different things make different people special.

Emphasise that when we recognise our differences and understand that it is OK to be different, we feel better about who we are. People who acknowledge their special characteristics, and accept these, generally have higher self-esteem.

Someone I admire (1)

Who do I admire?

Someone in my family

Someone famous

A friend of mine

Someone else

Someone I admire (2)

What makes this person special?

Something they are good at?

The way they look?

Something else

33

ACTIVITY 2.5

Participants are given and asked to individually complete the 'What makes me special?' sheets. First, participants identify their uniqueness in a variety of categories, for example, talents and skills ('Something I'm good at'), personal appearance ('Something about the way I look'), hobbies and interests ('Something I like to do'). Second, participants indicate ways in which one of these individual attributes or characteristics can be maximised or further developed ('What part of me can I make better?', 'What do I need to do?').

Responses are then presented to the rest of the group. This is a potential area for participants to follow up in collaboration with their support people.

Summary of Session 2

Today we have:

- talked about same and different
- said that there are many ways in which people can be different from each other
- seen that people can do things differently and that this is OK
- talked about recognising our differences and understanding that it is OK to be different. This is good for our self-esteem.

What makes me special? (1)

Something I'm good at

_____

Something about the way I look

_____

Something I like to do

_____

What makes me special? (2)

What part of me can I make better?

_____

What do I need to do?

_____

Session 3

Feeling Good

Aims of this session

1. Briefly review summary points from the last session.

2. Discuss some common feelings, ways we express them, and situations that evoke them.

3. Highlight that feelings can be similar, and also different, between individuals.

4. Explore the link between feelings and self-esteem.

Materials required

- Feelings cards.

- Feelings clock.

- 'My feelings' sheets.

Session plan

Briefly review summary points from the last session

> Facilitators should review the summary points from the last session.

Discuss some common feelings, ways we express them, and situations that evoke them

> Ask participants what they think is meant by 'feelings'. Emphasise that feelings are the different emotions and moods we experience inside. Ask participants to identify some feelings they have had (for example, happy, sad, excited, angry, frightened, proud, jealous). Emphasise that there are many different feelings but today we will focus on just some of these – happy, sad, angry, excited.

ACTIVITY 3.1

For this activity, participants first discuss ways of showing that we are happy, sad, angry and excited. The 'Feelings cards' are shown to participants one by one (each card should be cut out). The facilitator may need to obscure the bottom of the cards so as not to give away the answers when showing the cards to participants. First, ask participants to identify how the person in each picture is feeling. Second, ask participants to identify the eye, mouth and body characteristics associated with each feeling, for example, 'This person is feeling happy. How do we know the person is feeling happy? What is it about their eyes, mouth and body that tells you they are happy?'

Examples of responses include:

- happy (eyes wide open and shining, mouth smiling)
- sad (eyes small and turned down, lips turned down)
- angry (eyes small and pointed, mouth shut tight)
- excited (eyes extra wide open, mouth wide open).

Emphasise that we usually express feelings through our eyes and mouth, as well as our body.

Emphasise that different situations and people stir up certain feelings.

Feelings cards

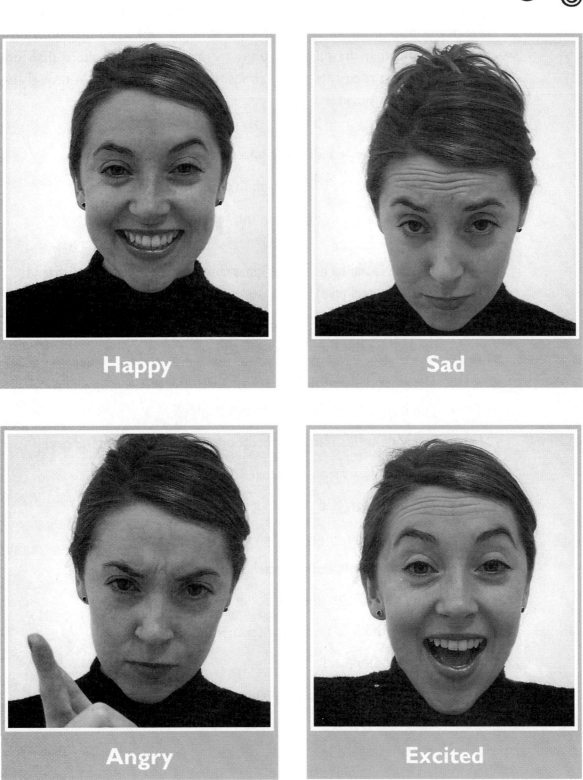

ACTIVITY 3.2

As a group activity, participants use the 'Feelings clock'. Each participant is given a turn. First, they are given a hypothetical situation. Then, they are asked to turn the clock hand to the feeling most strongly evoked by that situation.

Emphasise that in some situations we may experience more than one feeling, but that participants should choose the feeling that is most strongly associated with that situation.

Situations:

- Someone says a nice thing about your new jumper (happy).

- Someone cuts in front of you in a queue (angry).

- You are going to your favourite restaurant for dinner tonight (excited).

- You are ready to go to the cinema with a friend, and your friend calls to cancel (sad).

- You are waiting to pay for something in a store, and you are ignored by the shopkeeper (angry).

- You have had an argument with a friend (sad).

- You have just made a new friend (happy).

- Someone walks into your bedroom without knocking (angry).

- You have just seen a film that you enjoyed (happy).

- You have won first prize in a raffle (excited).

- You have your money stolen (angry).

- You lost your favourite watch (sad).

- You have bought yourself some new clothes (happy).

- Your birthday is tomorrow (excited).

- Your cat dies (sad).

- Your favourite friend is coming to stay at the weekend (excited).

Feelings clock

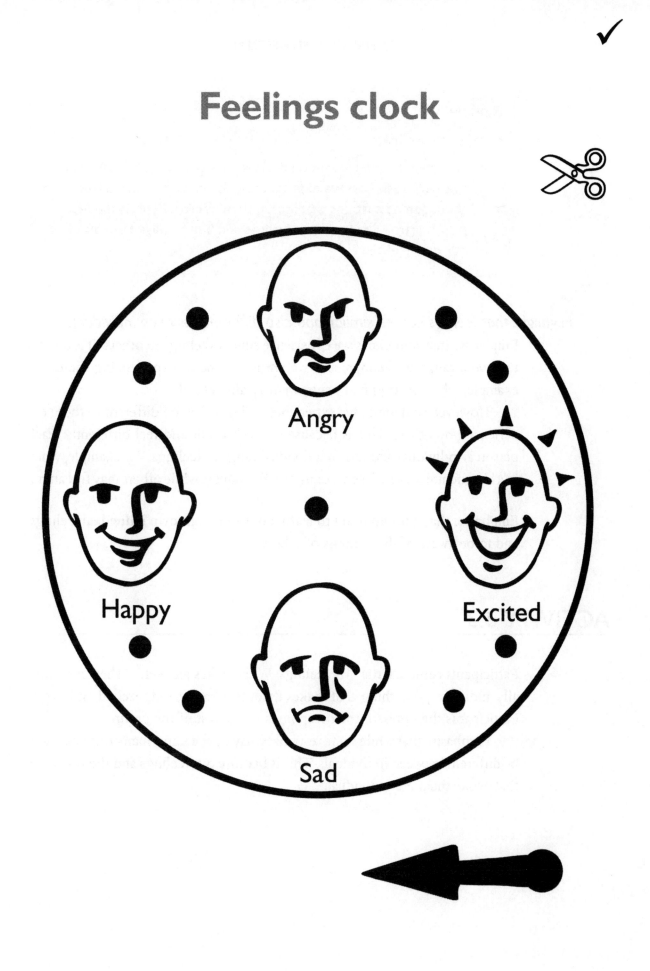

> **Review 3.1**
>
> So far today we have:
>
> - talked about some common feelings – happy, sad, angry, excited. We have seen how we express these feelings. We have talked about some situations that stir up these feelings. This is the first step in learning more about feelings and better ways to express our own feelings.

Highlight that feelings can be similar, and also different, between individuals

Emphasise that sometimes we experience similar feelings to others. It is normal to have a range of feelings, and we are not alone in experiencing these. For example, when hearing bad news, we may all feel sad.

However, sometimes we experience feelings that are different to those experienced by others. This is because we each think and feel differently. Each person is individual and has an individual range of feelings. For example, when in a big and noisy crowd, some of us may feel happy, while others may feel angry.

Emphasise that it is important to learn more about our own individual feelings, and to be aware of the feelings of others.

ACTIVITY 3.3

Participants complete the 'My feelings: What makes me feel...' sheet individually, indicating one thing that makes them feel happy, sad, excited and angry. Participants then present their responses to the rest of the group.

Emphasise that while some responses may be the same, many responses will be different between individuals. This is because our feelings and the situations that evoke them are individual.

My feelings: What makes me feel…

Happy

_____

_____

Sad

_____

_____

Angry

_____

_____

Excited

_____

_____

Review 3.2

So far today we have:

- talked about some common feelings – happy, sad, angry, excited. We have seen how we express these feelings. We have talked about some situations that stir up these feelings

- seen that we might feel the same as, but also different from others, and that some situations can stir up the same or different feelings in us. This shows that we each have an individual set of feelings.

Explore the link between feelings and self-esteem

Emphasise that nice feelings and high self-esteem go together. In general, the more nice feelings we have in our lives (happy, excited), the higher our self-esteem. Also, the higher our self-esteem, the more nice feelings we have.

Unpleasant feelings and low self-esteem go together. In general, the more unpleasant feelings we have in our lives (sad, angry), the lower our self-esteem.

Also, the lower our self-esteem, the more unpleasant feelings we have. Emphasise here that unpleasant feelings like sadness and anger are normal. Each of us feels sad and angry at different times in our lives. But when these unpleasant feelings start to run our lives, our self-esteem can really suffer.

How do we use our feelings to improve our self-esteem? We can try to increase pleasant feelings. We can also try to decrease unpleasant feelings. But we usually cannot get rid of unpleasant feelings totally – unpleasant feelings are a normal part of life. Sometimes we need to work on being able to cope better with unpleasant feelings.

ACTIVITY 3.4

Participants should now individually complete the 'My feelings: How can I feel...' sheet, indicating things that would make them more happy, less sad, less angry and more excited.

For happy and excited feelings, this will consist of attempting to do more of what makes the participant feel happy or excited (for example, if the participant has indicated they feel happy when following a football team, one suggestion may be that they attend more football matches).

For sad and angry feelings, this will consist of attempting to change the thing that makes the participant feel sad or angry (for example, if the participant has indicated they feel angry when in large crowds, one suggestion may be that they avoid crowded environments if possible). Also, for sad and angry feelings, it will be important to explore with participants adaptive (more helpful) ways of dealing with these feelings (for example, if the participant has indicated that they feel sad when they do not see their family for a week, one suggestion may be that they have an opportunity to talk with someone about this).

Re-emphasise that it is normal to experience a whole range of feelings, including feelings of sadness and anger. This is a potential area for participants to follow up in collaboration with their support people.

My feelings: How can I feel...

More
happy

_____

_____

Less
sad

_____

_____

Less
angry

_____

_____

More
excited

_____

_____

> **Summary of Session 3**
>
> Today we have:
>
> - talked about some common feelings – happy, sad, angry, excited. We have seen how we express these feelings. We have talked about some situations and people that stir up these feelings
>
> - seen that we might feel the same as others, but also different from others and that some situations can stir up the same or different feelings in us
>
> - seen that pleasant feelings go together with high self-esteem and unpleasant feelings go together with low self-esteem. We talked about ways to have more pleasant feelings, and less unpleasant feelings. This is so we can start to feel better about ourselves.

Session 4

Healthy Thinking

Aims of this session

1.   Briefly review summary points from the last session.

2.   Highlight the difference between positive thoughts and negative thoughts.

3.   Discuss how positive thoughts and negative thoughts impact on our self-esteem.

4.   Explore ways of utilising positive self-statements.

Materials required

- 'Positive and negative thoughts' boxes and cards.

- Dan and Bob thoughts charts.

- 'Negative thoughts' checklist.

- 'Thinking more positively' sheet.

Session plan

Briefly review summary points from the last session

Facilitators should review the summary points from the last session.

Highlight the difference between positive thoughts and negative thoughts

Emphasise that inside our heads, we all say things to ourselves. Some of the things we say to ourselves are nice things and good things. Ask participants if they can think of nice things and good things they say to themselves. Examples include 'I am a good person', 'I'm OK', or 'I can do this'. These types of thoughts are known as positive thoughts.

Inside our heads, some of the things we say to ourselves are awful and bad. Ask participants if they can think of awful and bad things they say to themselves. Examples include 'I'm a terrible person', 'I'm no good', or 'I can't do anything'. These types of thoughts are known as negative thoughts.

ACTIVITY 4.1

Facilitators cut out the positive and negative thoughts cards, as indicated. Each participant is asked to select a card from the comprising a self-talk statement (e.g. 'I am a nice person') and is asked to judge whether the statement is positive or negative. Participants sort their responses by putting the cards in the 'Positive and Negative thoughts' boxes (facilitators will need to construct the boxes for this activity, or alternatively, provide pre-constructed boxes). The self-talk statements appearing on the cards are summarised below.

Positive self-talk statements:

- I am a nice person
- I am a hard worker
- I am fun to be with
- I am proud of myself
- I am special
- I can handle this.

Negative self-talk statements:

- I am nothing special
- I am am not a good worker
- I am awful
- I am boring
- I can't do this
- I am not good at anything.

Positive and negative thoughts cards

I am a nice person

I am a hard worker

I am fun to be with

I am proud of myself

I am special

I can handle this

I am nothing special

I am not a good worker

I am awful

I am boring

I can't do this

I am not good at anything

Positive thoughts box

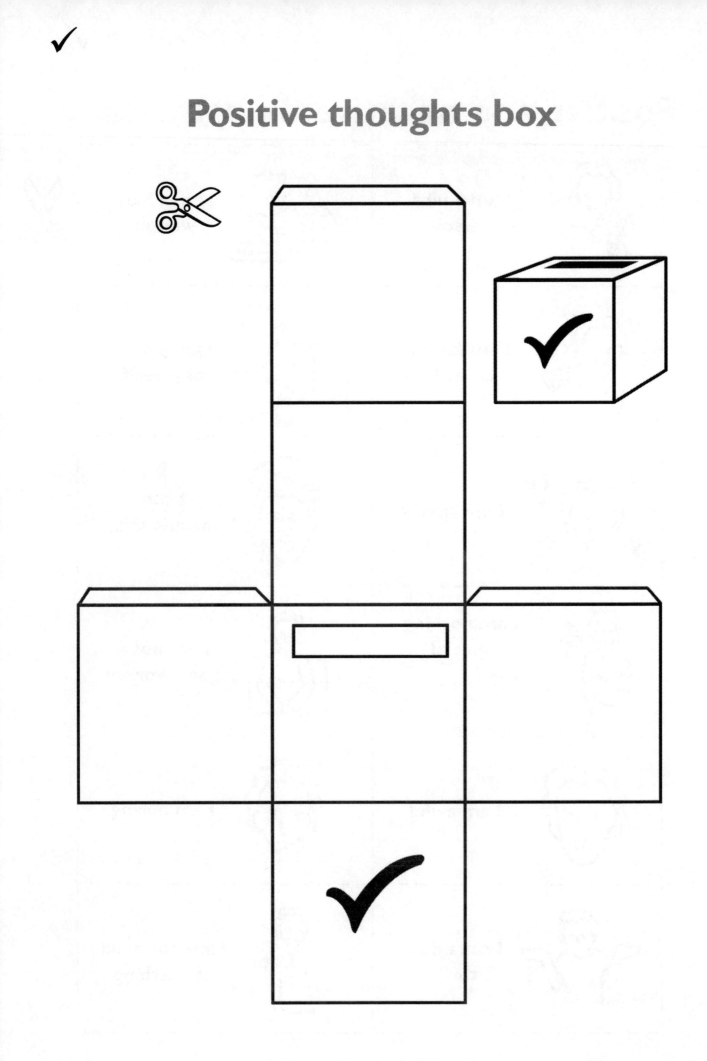

Negative thoughts box

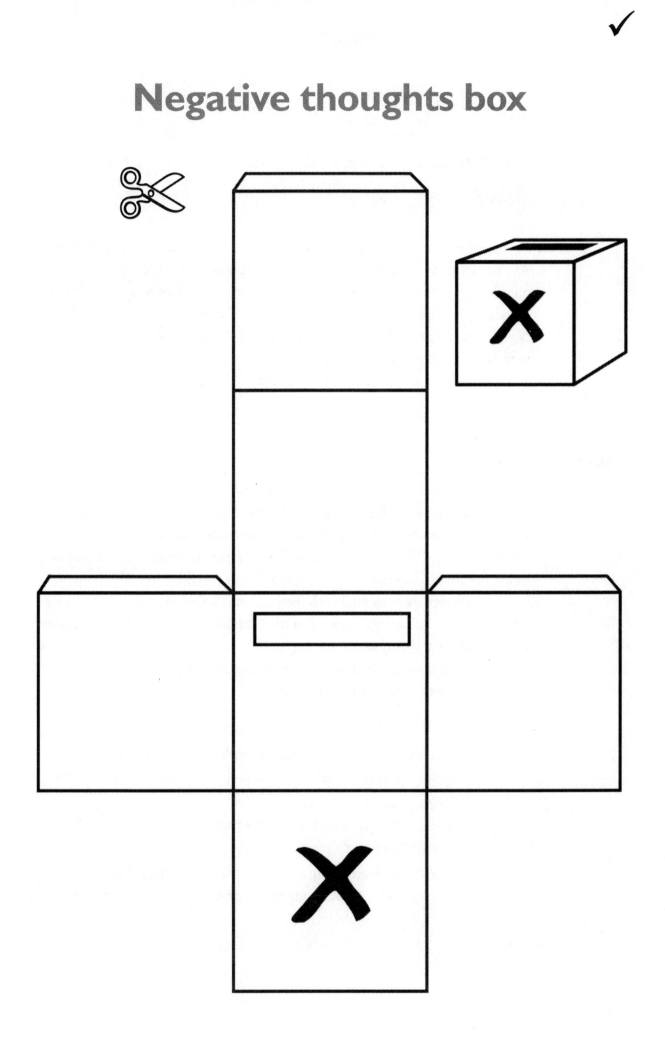

> **Review 4.1**
>
> So far today we have:
>
> - seen the difference between positive thoughts and negative thoughts. This is to help us be more aware of how we think.

Discuss how positive thoughts and negative thoughts impact on our self-esteem

Ask participants, 'When we think positive thoughts, how do we feel about ourselves?' Emphasise that positive thoughts help us feel good about ourselves. They give us a positive outlook and lift our self-esteem.

Ask participants, 'When we think negative thoughts, how do we feel about ourselves?' Emphasise that negative thoughts work against us. They give us a negative outlook and lower our self-esteem.

ACTIVITY 4.2

For this activity, participants discuss two hypothetical people, Dan and Bob. Using Dan's and Bob's thoughts charts, emphasise that Dan thinks positive thoughts such as 'I'm OK', 'I can do this', and 'I can get through this' while Bob thinks negative thoughts like 'I'm no good', 'I can't do this', and 'This is awful'.

Participants are presented with three situations (below) and asked to judge how Dan, then Bob, would cope with these situations. Emphasise that because Dan has positive thoughts, he has high self-esteem and is better able to cope with these situations; because Bob has negative thoughts, he has low self-esteem and is less able to cope with these situations.

Situations:

1.   Dan and Bob have a date set up with a friend. They are looking forward to this. At the last minute, the friend calls to cancel the date.

2.   Dan and Bob have just finished a painting. Someone says, 'That's an awful painting!'

3.   Dan and Bob are going to attend a large meeting. They have been asked to speak about an important issue at this meeting.

Dan's thoughts chart

I'm ok

I can do this

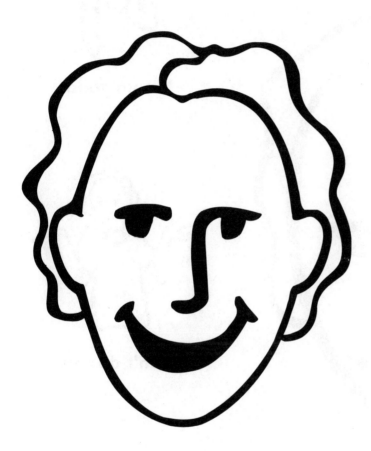

Dan

I can get through this

Bob's thoughts chart

Bob

I'm no good

I can't do this

This is awful

Review 4.2

So far today we have:

- seen the difference between positive thoughts and negative thoughts

- talked about how positive thoughts lift our self-esteem, while negative thoughts lower our self-esteem.

Explore ways of utilising positive self-statements

Emphasise that most of us have negative thoughts. However, we can send negative thoughts away and replace them with positive thoughts. This is not an easy thing to do, and it takes a lot of practice. But gradually we can shift from having negative thoughts to having more positive thoughts.

ACTIVITY 4.3

Individually, participants identify negative thoughts that they have had using the 'Negative thoughts Checklist' (ticking 'Yes' for thoughts they have had, and 'No' for thoughts they haven't had). Participants then present the negative thoughts that they have identified to the group. The group and facilitator help participants explore the situations in which they think that way (for example, 'When do you think you are no good?') and then discuss an alternative positive statement for handling that situation (for example, 'Even though I make mistakes, I'm still an OK person').

The new positive self-talk statements are written on the 'Thinking more positively' sheet. Participants are encouraged to make a cassette tape of these new positive self-talk statements and to listen to the tape each morning, as a healthy way to begin the day. This is a potential area for participants to follow up on in collaboration with their support people.

✓

I am no good ☐ Yes ☐ No

**I am not
a good worker** ☐ Yes ☐ No

I am awful to others ☐ Yes ☐ No

I am boring ☐ Yes ☐ No

Negative thoughts checklist (2)

I can't do this   ☐ Yes ☐ No

I am ugly   ☐ Yes ☐ No

I can't handle this   ☐ Yes ☐ No

I am a bad person   ☐ Yes ☐ No

Negative thoughts checklist (3)

I knew it would be bad ☐ Yes ☐ No

This is impossible ☐ Yes ☐ No

I will never get over this ☐ Yes ☐ No

I don't like being me ☐ Yes ☐ No

Thinking more positively

More positive thoughts I can have

_____

_____

_____

_____

_____

_____

_____

_____

_____

_____

Summary of Session 4

Today we have:

- seen the difference between positive thoughts and negative thoughts

- talked about how positive thoughts lift our self-esteem, while negative thoughts lower our self-esteem

- looked at ways we can have fewer negative thoughts and more positive thoughts.

For the next session, ask participants to bring a photo of themselves to the group.

Session 5

Accepting Who We Are

Aims of this session

1. Briefly review summary points from the last session.

2. Discuss what is meant by 'body' and 'body image' and how these relate to self-esteem.

3. Explore physical strengths and ways of maximising them, and explore physical limitations and ways of improving them.

4. Explore adjustment and acceptance of physical limitations that we cannot change.

Materials required

- Person puzzle.

- 'Number of people who feel negatively about their body' chart.

- 'Guess who?' sheet.

- Photo of each participant (each participant to provide).

- 'What I like about me' sheet.

- 'My body' checklist.

- 'Coping with limitations tips' sheet.

Session plan

Briefly review summary points from the last session

Facilitators should review the summary points from the last session.

Discuss what is meant by 'body' and 'body image' and how these relate to self-esteem

Ask participants what our bodies are made up of. Emphasise that our bodies are made up of body parts (for example, head, arms, legs), body features (for example, colour of hair, eyes and skin, height, weight) and other things to do with our bodies (for example, hairstyle, beard, glasses, clothing).

ACTIVITY 5.1

Cut out all the pieces of the 'Person puzzle' for this activity. Participants are asked to select a puzzle piece, name the body part selected, and place the piece in the right position in the puzzle to make the person again. Emphasise that our body is made of many different components.

Ask participants what is meant by body image. Emphasise that body image is how we view our bodies. We have a good body image when we like and accept our bodies. People who feel like this tend to have higher self-esteem. We have a poor body image when we do not like and reject our bodies. People who feel like this tend to have lower self-esteem. In fact, it is suggested that about one in three people do not like their looks (Frank and Edwards 1988).

Person puzzle

65

ACTIVITY 5.2

Display 'Number of people who feel negatively about their body' chart. Emphasise that one in three people report feeling negatively about their body – feeling negative is quite common and it is important for people to start feeling better about their bodies.

Number of people who feel negatively about their body

I in 3 people

Review 5.1

So far today we have:

- seen what is meant by 'body'. We also talked about what is meant by 'body image' and how this works together with self-esteem.

Explore physical strengths and ways of maximising them, and explore physical limitations and ways of improving them

Emphasise that our bodies can be similar to, and different from, the bodies of others.

Ask participants how our bodies are similar to others. Emphasise that all of us share some common body features, such as legs, head etc.

Ask participants how our bodies are different to others.

Emphasise that each of us has body features that are unique and special to us, such as types of hair, eye colour, height, weight etc.

ACTIVITY 5.3

Each participant individually circles their hair colour, hair style and any distinguishing features (for example, glasses) on the 'Guess Who?' sheet. Participants hand in the completed sheet to the facilitator.

For each sheet, the facilitator reads out the list of characteristics (for example, 'this person has brown, long, curly hair') and participants are asked to guess the person being described.

Guess who?

Hair colour **Brown** **Blonde** **Black** **Other**

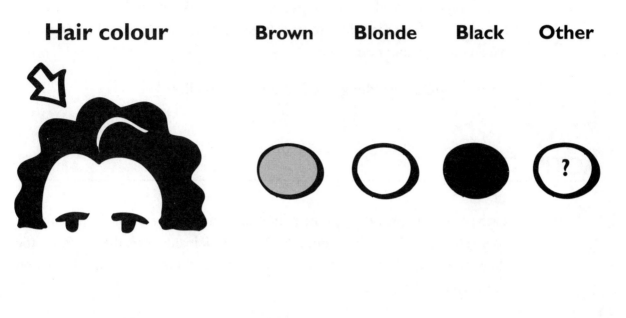

Hair style **Straight** **Curly** **Long** **Short**

Special features **Glasses** **Earring** **Hat** **Other**

We have seen that each of our bodies is special or one of a kind. For a lot of us, there are things we like about our bodies. For example, we may feel we have nice hair. Also, for a lot of us, there are things we do not like about our bodies. For example, we may feel we are overweight. When it comes to our bodies, we all have things that we like, and things that we do not like. We will now spend some time talking about the things that we like about our bodies, and the things that we do not like about our bodies.

First, we will discuss things we like about our bodies.

ACTIVITY 5.4

Each participant provides a photo of himself or herself. Participants individually complete the 'What I like about me' sheet. Participants stick the photo on the sheet, then identify two body strengths. Participants present their information to the rest of the group.

What I like about me

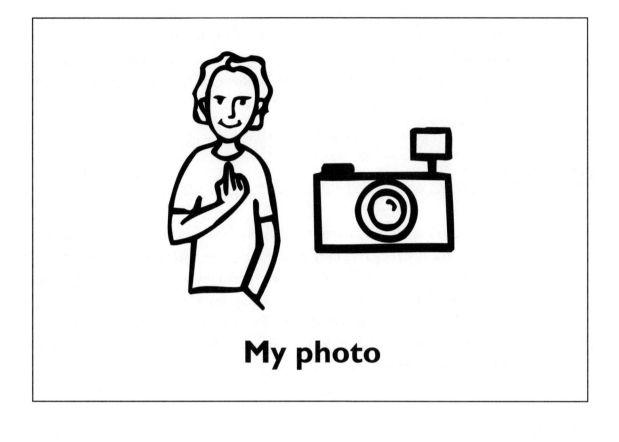

My photo

Two things I like about my body

_____

_____

We have seen there are many things about our bodies that we like. But for many of us, there are also some things about our bodies that we do not like. Let's talk about some of these.

There are some things we do not like about our bodies that we can improve. Ask participants whether they can think of any things they do not like about their bodies that they can improve or change. Examples include our complexion, hairstyle, weight, clothing etc. Emphasise that everyone can set goals to improve things about their bodies they do not like.

ACTIVITY 5.5

Participants individually complete the 'My body checklist'. First, participants identify whether they feel they need to improve their physical characteristics according to the categories of clothing, hairstyle, weight, grooming or other areas. Second, if an affirmative response is indicated in any one of these categories, realistic goals are set individually for achieving this improvement.

This is a potential area for participants to follow up in collaboration with their support people.

My body checklist

What I'd like to make better

My clothes   **My hair**   **My weight**   **My grooming**   **Other areas**

How can I make these better?

_____

_____

> **Review 5.2**
>
> So far today we have:
>
> - seen what is meant by 'body'. We also talked about what is meant by 'body image' and how this works together with self-esteem
>
> - talked about things we like about our bodies and ways to make the most of them. Also, we talked about things we do not like about our bodies and that we can change.

Explore adjustment and acceptance of physical limitations that we cannot change

We said before that there are some things about our bodies that we do not like. Some of these things we can change. But some of these things we cannot change. Emphasise there are some things we do not like about our bodies that we can't do much about. Ask participants whether they can think of any things they do not like about their bodies that they can't change. Examples include differences in our bodies we can't help, such as those associated with disability.

Emphasise that everyone has limitations that they can't change. It is important that we think about ways of adjusting or accepting some of our limitations. This may be more difficult for some than for others because of the types of limitations they have, and the impact of these limitations on their life. Also, different people may need a different amount of time and support (for example, counselling) to deal with this issue.

ACTIVITY 5.6

Participants are first asked to identify helpful strategies they can use to cope with disability. Participants are then presented with the 'Coping with limitations tips' sheet. Participants are encouraged to use helpful strategies in coping with disability issues. This is a potential area for participants to follow up in collaboration with their support people.

Coping with limitations tips

**Focus on the things
I can do**

**Try things a
different way**

**Talk to someone who
understands**

**Talk to someone in a
similar situation**

Summary of Session 5

Today we have:

- seen what is meant by 'body'. We also talked about what is meant by 'body image', and how this works together with self-esteem

- talked about things we like about our bodies and ways to make the most of these things. Also, we talked about things we do not like about our bodies and that we can change

- talked about things we do not like about our bodies and need to work on accepting.

Session 6

Speaking up
for Ourselves

Aims of this session

1.   Briefly review summary points from the last session.

2.   Explore why being assertive is important to our self-esteem.

3.   Highlight the difference between passive, assertive and aggressive behaviour styles.

4.   Explore techniques for assertive behaviour.

5.   Identify situations in which participants behave non-assertively.

6.   Explore ways that participants can be more assertive in these situations.

Materials required

- Passive, assertive, aggressive cards.

- Situation cards.

- 'Assertive behaviour tips' sheet.

- Assertiveness questionnaire.

- 'Being more assertive' sheet.

Session plan

Briefly review summary points from the last session

Facilitators should review the summary points from the last session.

Explore why being assertive is important to our self-esteem

Ask participants what it means to be assertive. Emphasise that being assertive means to stand up for yourself, your rights and your beliefs, in a responsible way. We will discuss this in more detail later. Ask participants why being assertive is important to our self-esteem. Emphasise that being assertive can help our self-esteem by:

- giving us a greater sense of control in our lives (if we stand up for ourselves, we are more likely to get our needs met)

- giving us more self-confidence

- getting us respect from others because we have the courage to take a stand.

Review 6.1

So far today we have:

- talked about how being assertive helps our self-esteem. We said that speaking up for ourselves can help us feel good about ourselves.

Highlight the difference between passive, assertive and aggressive behaviour styles

The first step to being more assertive is to better understand what assertive behaviour is.

In living and communicating with others, we behave in many different ways. Sometimes we fail to speak up. An example of this is when we do not say 'no' to people when we really feel like saying 'no'. This can make us feel awful and feel that we have been unfairly treated. This sort of behaviour is known as being 'passive' or being 'meek'.

Sometimes we feel that the only way we can get our needs met is to be demanding or difficult. An example of this is when we yell at other people when we want something. This can make others feel awful and as if they have been unfairly treated. This sort of behaviour is known as being 'aggressive' or 'pushy'.

But there is another way we can express ourselves, without being passive or aggressive. This is known as being assertive. When we are assertive, we speak up for ourselves, but in a way that is fair on us and fair on others. An example of assertive behaviour is when we say 'no' to people when we feel like saying 'no'. Another example of assertive behaviour is letting someone know we want something while staying calm and not getting angry.

ACTIVITY 6.1

A 'problem' scenario is presented (see below). Passive, assertive and aggressive behaviour responses to this scenario are role-played by the facilitator (see table). The facilitator uses the 'Passive, assertive and aggressive cards' (which need to be cut out as indicated) to indicate which response style he or she is displaying.

Problem scenario:

A shopkeeper gives you the wrong change – he has given you less change than you should have.

Response style	Response
Passive	Do not say anything, and walk away
Aggressive	Start yelling, 'How dare you give me the wrong change. You are a fool. Give me the right change now!'
Assertive	Calmly say, 'Excuse me, you gave me the wrong amount of change.'

Passive, assertive, agressive cards

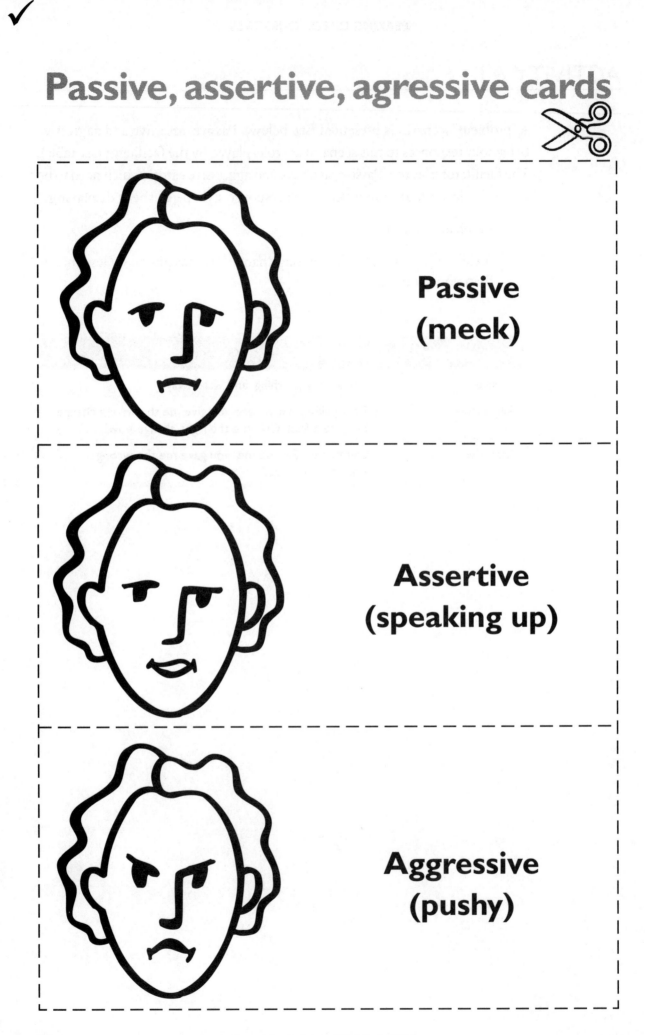

**Passive
(meek)**

**Assertive
(speaking up)**

**Aggressive
(pushy)**

We will now do another activity to help us understand the difference between passive, assertive and aggressive behaviour better.

ACTIVITY 6.2

Participants role-play one of three interpersonal situations involving either a passive, aggressive or assertive response style.

Interpersonal Situation	Response	Response style
You are sitting on the couch. Someone says, 'Get off – I want to sit there.'	You get off, and do not speak up.	Passive
Your house-mate makes a mess.	You say, 'You're an idiot. Clean up or move out.'	Aggressive
Someone touches your body. You don't like it.	You say, 'Don't touch me.'	Assertive

One participant at a time selects a Situation card and is helped to role-play the scenario represented on this card. The other participants are asked to judge which style of behaviour is being used. Participants indicate their judgement by showing the Passive, assertive and aggressive cards used in the previous exercise.

Passive situation card

You are sitting on the couch.

Someone says, 'Get off, I want to sit there!!'

You get off and don't speak up.

Aggressive situation card

Your house-mate makes a mess.

You say, 'You're an idiot. Clean up or move out.'

Assertive situation card

Someone touches your body.

You don't like it.

You say, 'Don't touch me!'

Review 6.2

So far today we have:

- talked about how being assertive is important to our self-esteem

- talked about the difference between passive, assertive and aggressive behaviour. We learned about three different ways people can behave in situations.

Explore techniques for assertive behaviour

Ask participants how we show we are assertive. Emphasise that we can:

- use our voice (or other form of communication) to tell people what we want or do not want (for example, 'I want…' or 'I do not want…')

- make eye contact

- use gestures

- keep a good posture.

All these things let others know what we want or what we do not want.

ACTIVITY 6.3

Hand out the 'Assertive behaviour tips' sheet and review each of the tips presented on this sheet. Have one participant volunteer an example of an interpersonal situation that they have had difficulty managing, such as a situation that involved confrontation. Then support this participant in role-playing an assertive response to this situation, employing the strategies outlined in the 'Assertiveness behaviour tips' sheet. Have other participants identify the types of assertive behaviours shown by the participant during the role-play.

Assertive behaviour tips

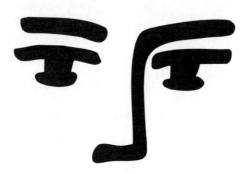

Look at the person

Tell people what you want or what you don't want

Sit or stand up straight

Use gestures

Review 6.3

Today we have:

- talked about how being assertive is important to our self-esteem
- talked about the difference between passive, assertive and aggressive behaviour
- talked about assertive behaviour, and seen some examples of people being assertive. This is to help us learn more about what being assertive means.

Identify situations in which participants behave non-assertively

For each of us, there are situations where we do not behave assertively. In other words, there may be situations where we do not speak up for ourselves, and we are passive or meek. There may also be situations when we walk all over others, and we are aggressive or pushy. We will now complete an activity that will help us look at our own behaviour, and help us identify situations in which we do not behave assertively.

ACTIVITY 6.4

Participants individually complete the 'Assertiveness questionnaire'. The facilitator asks each participant to share one situation identified from the questionnaire where they behave assertively, and reinforces the example of assertive behaviour. The facilitator then asks each participant to share one situation where they do not behave assertively, and explores these instances of non-assertive behaviour with the participant.

Emphasise that non-assertive behaviour can be changed. Emphasise that in some instances, participants may choose to behave non-assertively (for example, in order to not hurt the feelings of a close friend). We do not have to be assertive all the time – just for the important things. Note that what is considered to be *important* will depend on the individual, and on the situation they are in.

Assertiveness questionnaire (1)

Are you assertive when:

speaking up about problems? ☐ Yes ☐ No

talking in a group? ☐ Yes ☐ No

handling negative comments? ☐ Yes ☐ No

Assertiveness questionnaire (2)

Are you assertive when:

asking for help?   ☐ Yes ☐ No

saying 'No'?   ☐ Yes ☐ No

asking questions?   ☐ Yes ☐ No

Assertiveness questionnaire (3)

Are you assertive with:

family?   ☐ Yes   ☐ No

friends?   ☐ Yes   ☐ No

staff?   ☐ Yes   ☐ No

professionals (such as doctors)?   ☐ Yes   ☐ No

Ask participants why it is that sometimes when we want to be assertive, we do not behave assertively. Emphasise that this is usually because we are shy or we feel too frightened to speak up. While these feelings are normal, it is important to remember you have a right to speak up for yourself. If you feel you cannot speak up on your own, you can ask for help (for example, from a friend or an advocate).

Review 6.4

Today we have:

- talked about how being assertive is important to our self-esteem

- talked about the difference between passive, assertive and aggressive behaviour

- talked about assertive behaviour, and seen some examples of people being assertive

- looked at situations where each of us do and do not behave assertively. This is to help us learn more about our own style of behaviour.

Explore ways that participants can be more assertive in these situations
We will now look at ways in which we can behave more assertively.

ACTIVITY 6.5

Participants complete the 'Being more assertive' sheet as a group exercise, drawing on information from the 'Assertiveness questionnaire' used in the previous activity (pp.88–90). Participants provide a response to the question, 'How will I be more assertive?'

This is a potential area for the participant to follow up in collaboration with their support person.

Being more assertive

How will I be more assertive?

_____

_____

_____

_____

_____

_____

_____

_____

_____

_____

_____

Summary of Session 6

Today we have:

- talked about how being assertive is important to our self-esteem

- talked about the difference between passive, assertive and aggressive behaviour

- talked about assertive behaviour, and seen some examples of people being assertive

- looked at situations where each of us do and do not behave assertively

- looked at ways we can each behave more assertively and have more control over our own lives.

Session 7

Communicating Well

Aims of this session

1. Briefly review summary points from the last session.
2. Discuss the importance of good communication skills to self-esteem.
3. Explore listening skills.
4. Explore conversation skills.

Materials required

- 'Good communication tips' sheets.

Session plan

Briefly review summary points from the last session

Facilitators should review the summary points from the last session.

Discuss the importance of good communication skills to self-esteem

Ask participants what is meant by good communication skills. Emphasise that good communication skills are the skills that help us communicate with others. There are many types of communication skills. Today we will talk about two types: listening and conversation skills.

Ask participants why good communication skills are important to our self-esteem. Emphasise that good communication skills help us to lead more fulfilling lives, and allow us to enjoy other people, different opportunities, and different experiences.

For this reason and many others, good communication skills are important to our self-esteem.

> **Review 7.1**
>
> So far today we have:
>
> - seen that good communication skills are important for our self-esteem. Good communication helps us to participate in groups.

Explore listening skills

Ask participants what is meant by listening skills. Emphasise that listening means we pay attention to someone when they are communicating with us. By doing this, we can find out a lot of important information. We also show that we are interested in what the other person is saying.

Ask participants how we show that we are listening. Emphasise that we show we are listening by looking at the other person we are talking with. Ask participants how else we show that we are listening. Emphasise we can show we are listening by nodding when we understand what the person is saying, and smiling when we like what the person is saying.

ACTIVITY 7.1

The facilitator asks one participant a casual question (for example, 'What are your favourite foods?'). While the participant is responding, the facilitator does not make eye contact, and does not nod their head or smile. Participants are asked, 'What am I doing wrong?', 'How does (the speaker) feel?', 'How do I do it correctly?'

The facilitator repeats the casual question, this time looking, nodding and smiling appropriately. Participants are then asked to practise asking each other casual questions (for example, 'What are your favourite hobbies?', 'What do you like to do in your spare time?'), using the listening strategies discussed (looking, nodding and smiling).

Participants are given the 'Good communication tips (listening)' sheet, which summarises the main features of listening skills.

Good communication tips: listening

Look at others when they are speaking with you

Smile if you are happy with what others are saying

Nod if you understand what others are saying

Review 7.2

So far today we have:

- seen that good communication skills are important for our self-esteem

- learned that it is important to listen to others when they are speaking with us. This is so that we can find out information, and show that we are interested in what the person is saying.

Explore conversation skills

Ask participants what we mean by conversation skills. Emphasise that conversation skills are used when we want to start a conversation, keep a conversation going, or end a conversation. By doing this, we can enjoy the company of other people. Ask participants how we can start a conversation. Emphasise that when we want to start a conversation, it is important to:

- wait for the right time to start a conversation – make sure the person is available to speak with you, and is not talking with someone else

- let the person know what it is you want to talk about

- use an appropriate greeting, such as 'Hello' or 'Excuse me'.

Ask participants how we can keep a conversation going. Emphasise that when we want to keep a conversation going, it is important to:

- keep on the topic and stick to what is being discussed

- listen to the other person, using the listening skills we have just discussed

- share the conversation, making sure not to take over. Let the other person have a say, as well as you.

Ask participants how we can end a conversation. Emphasise that when we want to end a conversation, it is important to:

- choose the right time to end a conversation. Do not end the conversation when someone is talking about something important or is in the middle of a sentence. End the conversation when it seems as though the other person has finished what they have to say and is ready to leave.

- use an appropriate end-statement, such as, 'Thanks for talking with me.' or 'See you later.'

Now we will practise putting our conversation skills in place.

ACTIVITY 7.2

Three participants are asked to volunteer for a role-play. For this role-play, two participants are busy talking about their weekend. The third participant approaches the other two and says, 'I didn't like the camp!' and leaves. The facilitator asks the group, 'What did the (person) do wrong?' and whether the person:

- waited for the right time to start the conversation

- let the others know what it was he wanted to talk about

- used a greeting

- kept on the topic

- listened to the others

- chose the right time to end the conversation

- used an appropriate end-statement.

Participants are given the 'Good communication tips' (starting a conversation, keeping a conversation going, ending a conversation) sheets, which summarise the main features of good conversation skills.

The facilitator reviews the information on this sheet with participants. The role-play is repeated, but this time the third participant handles the conversation correctly and follows each of the above steps.

Summary of Session 7

Today we have:

- seen that good communication skills are important for our self-esteem

- learned that it is important to listen to others when they are speaking with us

- discussed some of the important points to starting, continuing and ending a conversation. This is to help us have better conversations with others.

Good communication tips: starting a conversation

 **Wait for the right time to start**

 **Let the person know what you want to talk about**

 **Use a greeting, such as 'Hello'**

Good communication tips: keeping a conversation going

 **Stick to the topic**

 **Take turns with speaking and listening**

 **Listen to the other person**

Good communication tips: ending a conversation

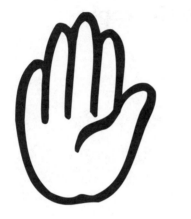

Wait for the right time to end

Finish the conversation; say 'Goodbye'

Session 8

Handling Problems

Aims of this session

1. Briefly review summary points from the last session.
2. Identify the sorts of problems we can experience and how they can affect our self-esteem.
3. Explore helpful and unhelpful ways of handling problems.
4. Discuss problem solving strategies.

Materials required

- 'A problem I've had' sheet.
- Problem scenario cards.
- 'Problem solving tips' sheet.

Session plan

Briefly review summary points from the last session

Facilitators should review the summary points from the last session.

Identify the sorts of problems we can experience and how they can affect our self-esteem

Ask participants what is meant by problems. Emphasise that problems are the difficulties we face in our day-to-day lives. We can face problems at home, at work and at services we use. We can face problems with family members, friends, people we know and people in the community.

Problems are a normal part of life. Everyone experiences problems at certain times in their life. Ask participants whether they know anyone who has never had a problem in their life. Obviously, the answer here is 'no'.

Emphasise that all of us experience problems from time to time. However, when we have too many problems in our life, or if we can not solve the problems we are experiencing, our self-esteem may suffer. We can start feeling bad about ourselves.

ACTIVITY 8.1

Participants use the 'A problem I've had' sheet to identify a problem they have experienced and how it affected the way they felt. Emphasise that each of us experiences problems from time to time, and that experiencing some problems is a normal part of life. Emphasise that when we have problems, we usually do not feel good about ourselves.

Note: the aim of this exercise is for participants to identify a problem that is appropriate for discussion in a group context and can be shared with others. The facilitator will need to ensure that issues of a sensitive nature are re-directed.

A problem I've had

A problem I had:

How did I feel?

Frustrated   **Angry**   **Sad**   **Scared**   **Other**

Review 8.1

So far today we have:

- learned that we can each experience problems. When we experience problems, this can affect the way we feel about ourselves.

Explore helpful and unhelpful ways of handling problems

When it comes to problems, there are helpful and unhelpful ways of handling them. Helpful ways are things we can do that help us to solve the problem. Unhelpful ways are things we can do that do not help us to solve the problem, and that sometimes make things worse. Let's look at the difference between helpful and unhelpful ways of handling problems.

ACTIVITY 8.2

For this activity, role-play is used to demonstrate the difference between helpful and unhelpful ways of handling problems.

A participant is presented with one of the 'Problem scenario' cards, and is supported first to role-play the helpful response to the situation, then the unhelpful response. The rest of the group observes the role-play and is asked to identify which of the responses was helpful, and which was unhelpful. Scenarios and responses to be role-played are included on the 'Problem scenario' cards: dealing with criticism; dealing with disagreements; dealing with disaapointments.

Problem scenario card:
dealing with criticism

**You've just had a haircut.
Someone says, 'That looks awful.'**

 **Helpful**

You say, 'I don't agree, I like it.'

 **Unhelpful**

You say, 'I think you look stupid.'

✓

Problem scenario card: dealing with disagreements

You're watching your favourite TV show

Your house-mate changes the channel

Helpful   You say, 'Let's tape one of the shows.'

Unhelpful   You say, 'I hate you.'

Problem scenario card: dealing with disappointment

You want to go to the movies

No one can assist you to go

Helpful

You try to find someone to take you tomorrow

Unhelpful

You start kicking and screaming

> **Review 8.2**
>
> So far today we have:
>
> - learned that we can each experience problems. When we experience problems, this can affect the way we feel about ourselves
>
> - talked about helpful and unhelpful ways of handling problems. This is so we can better understand the difference between helpful and unhelpful ways.

Discuss problem solving strategies

When we face a problem, it is often helpful to try to solve it. There are a number of steps we can take to try to solve the problems we face. These steps are outlined below:

1. Find out what the problem is – be clear about the problem and what is happening in the situation you are faced with.

2. Think about some of the things you can do to solve the problem – usually there are many choices you can make.

3. From all these choices, work out which one is the best – choose the thing that will help you to get what you want, without causing any further problems for you or others.

4. Try it out and see how it goes – if it works, continue with it. If it does not, then try another way of solving the problem.

ACTIVITY 8.3

Use the scenarios outlined on the 'Problem scenario cards' (from the previous activity) and listed below:

- You've just had a haircut. Someone says, 'That looks awful.'

- You're watching your favourite TV show. Your house-mate changes the channel.

- You want to go to the movies. No one can assist you to you.

Help participants to identify the possible steps in solving each of these problems, using the 'Problem solving tips' sheet.

Problem solving tips

Work out what the problem is

Work out what you can do

Choose the best thing to do

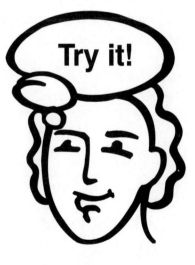

Try it and see

Summary of Session 8

So far today we have:

- learned that we can each experience problems. When we experience problems, this can affect the way we feel about ourselves

- talked about helpful and unhelpful ways of handling problems

- talked about some steps we can use to solve problems. This was to show us a helpful way of handling problems.

For the next session, ask participants to bring with them an item that represents a special achievement (for example, a photo or a certificate).

Session 9

Reaching our Goals

Aims of this session

1. Briefly review summary points from the last session.
2. Explore the link between achievements, goals and self-esteem.
3. Discuss past achievements.
4. Discuss goals for the future.

Materials required

- An item that represents a special achievement (for example, photo, certificate) to be brought in by each participant.
- 'My achievement' sheet.
- 'My goal' sheet.

Session plan

Briefly review summary points from the last session

Facilitators should review the summary points from the last session.

Explore the link between achievements, goals and self-esteem

Ask participants what is meant by achievements. Emphasise that achievements are things we have done in the past that we are proud of. Achievements may include:

- learning to travel independently
- learning to use a computer
- developing better communication skills
- attending a meeting to represent the people you work with.

Ask participants why it is important to focus on our achievements. Emphasise that achievements generally require us to put in a great deal of effort (for example, learning to use a computer requires a lot of practice, time, dedication and self-discipline). By focusing on our achievements, we are acknowledging our hard work. When we focus on our achievements, our self-esteem grows.

Ask participants what is meant by goals. Emphasise that goals are things we hope to do in future. Goals may include:

- improving shopping skills

- becoming more confident when speaking in front of a group

- going on a holiday

- handling money more independently.

Ask participants why it is important to focus on goals. Emphasise that goals give us something to aim for in the future. By setting goals, we are working towards improving ourselves. When we have goals, our self-esteem grows.

Review 9.1

So far today we have:

- seen that it is important to focus on our achievements and goals, and that this is good for our self-esteem.

Discuss past achievements

It is important to focus on our achievements – we should be proud of the good things we have done in the past. Occasionally, it is nice to give ourselves a 'pat on the back'.

ACTIVITY 9.1

Participants should bring in an item that represents one of their valued achievements (for example, an award they have received, a photo of them involved in a special activity, an item they have made).

Each participant individually completes a 'My achievement' sheet in relation to this valued achievement. Participants provide information under the categories of 'What did I achieve?', 'When did I achieve this?', 'Why am I proud of this?' Participants are facilitated to present their items and responses to the group.

My achievement

What did I achieve?

When did I achieve this?

Why am I proud of this?

Review 9.2

So far today we have:

- seen that focusing on our achievements and setting goals is important to our self-esteem

- talked about one of our special achievements. It is important to be proud of some of the good things we have achieved in the past.

Discuss goals for the future:

Emphasise that while it is important to focus on past achievements, it is also important to set goals for the future. We need to continue to set our sights on something and to go after it.

Emphasise that a goal can be something that everybody can see (for example, losing two kilograms), or something that is more private (for example, getting along better with your family, overcoming shyness). Ask participants what types of goals they are already working on. Ask participants what sorts of things get in the way of achieving goals.

Emphasise that fear is one of the many things that can get in the way of achieving goals. Emphasise that while fear is normal, it is important to keep in mind that sometimes we need to 'give it a go' (provided it is safe to do so). Also, even if we do not achieve what we set out to do, just putting in the effort can be a good thing in itself.

Each person can set his or her own goals. There are certain things we can put in place to make it more likely we will reach our goals.

- Make your goal as specific as possible – for example, rather than saying, 'I want to have more fun', saying, 'I want to go to the movies once a month'.

- Write your goal down – we will do this in a moment.

- Try to set one important goal at a time.

- Give yourself a date to reach your goal by.

- Try to break your goals into steps, and try to achieve one step at a time – for example, if you want to buy a TV, putting away $10 a week; if you want to travel in the community more independently, riding public transport once a week.

- Set goals that you are able to reach.

ACTIVITY 9.2

Participants complete the 'My goal' sheet individually. Information is provided under a range of categories ('What is my goal?', 'When will I do this by?', 'What do I need to do?'). The information is then discussed with the group. This is a potential area for participants to follow up in collaboration with their support people.

Summary of Session 9

Today we have:

- seen that focusing on our achievements and setting goals is important to our self-esteem

- talked about one of our special achievements

- talked about one of our goals for the future. We put together a plan for reaching our goal.

My goal

What is my goal?

When will I do this by?

What do I need to do?

Session 10

Putting it all Together

Aims of this session

1. Briefly review summary points from the last session.
2. Provide an overview of information covered in sessions, evaluate skills developed and identify any areas of continued need.

Materials required

- 'Self-esteem evaluation' sheet.
- Certificate of achievement.

Session plan

Briefly review summary points from the last session

Facilitators should review the summary points from the last session.

Provide an overview of information covered in sessions, evaluate skills developed and identify any areas of continued need

Emphasise that over the sessions, we have talked about many things and have done activities to help us feel better about ourselves. We have talked about things that are important to our self-esteem. These were:

- what is self-esteem?
- what makes us special?
- feeling good
- healthy thinking
- accepting who we are
- speaking up for ourselves
- communicating well
- handling problems
- reaching our goals.

ACTIVITY 10.1

Participants complete the 'Self-esteem evaluation' sheet. As part of this, participants tick 'Yes' for areas where they feel that their knowledge/skills have developed since commencing the course', and 'Need more worok' for areas where they feel that their knowledge/skills need to be developed further. Participants then come together and discuss their responses.

The facilitator can use this opportunity to do the following:

- Reflect and recap on the specific skills covered in the course – for example, 'So, who remembers what we leaned about when we talked about feelings?'

- Explore instances of skill acquisition – for example, 'Who feels they now know more about feelings?', and acknowledge this positive progress.

- Explore areas of continued need – for example, 'Who feels they still need to learn more about feelings?', and specific follow-up to address these needs. This is a potential area for participants to follow up in collaboration with their support people.

Self-esteem evaluation

Session	Area of knowledge/skill	Yes	Need more work
1. **What is self-esteem?**	I know what self-esteem is.		
	I know why high self-esteem is important.		
2. **What makes us special?**	I can recognise what makes me special.		
	I know how to make the most of the things that make me special.		
3. **Feeling good**	I know about different feelings.		
	I know what to do to have more good feelings.		
	I know what to do to have less bad feelings.		
4. **Healthy thinking**	I know the difference between positive and negative thoughts.		
	I have identified some of my own negative thoughts.		
	I have some ideas on how to have more positive thoughts.		
5. **Accepting who we are**	I know bodies are made up of a lot of different parts.		
	I know each of our bodies is different.		
	I know the things I like about my body, and ways to make the most of these.		
6. **Speaking up for ourselves**	I know the difference between passive, assertive and aggressive behaviour.		
	I know about situations where I am not assertive.		
	I have some ideas on how I can be more assertive.		
7. **Communicating well**	I know how to listen when communicating with others.		
	I know how to handle a conversation better.		
8. **Handling problems**	I know the difference between helpful and unhelpful ways of dealing with problems.		
	I know some helpful ways for dealing with problems.		
9. **Reaching our goals**	I know some past achievements.		
	I have set some goals for the future.		
	I have some ideas on how to reach these goals.		

ACTIVITY 10.2

Participants are individually presented with their 'Certificate of Achievement'.

Summary of Session 10

Today we have:

- reviewed the information we covered in all the sessions. We have looked at the sorts of things we learned and the sorts of things we can continue to work on.

Certificate of achievement

_____

Name

has completed the self-esteem programme

_____

Signature

_____

Date

_____

Signature

_____

Date

References

Canfield, J. and Wells, H.C. (1976) *100 Ways to Enhance Self-concept in the Classroom: A Handbook for Teachers and Parents*. New Jersey: Prentice-Hall.

Frank, R.A. and Edwards, J.P. (1988) *Building Self-esteem in Persons with Developmental Disabilities*. Portland, OR: Ednick Communications.

Kriegsman, K.H., Zaslow, E.I. and D'Zmura-Rechsteiner (1992) *Taking Charge: Teenagers Talk about Life and Physical Disabilities*. New York: Woodbine House Inc.

Tonks, L. (1990) *I Think, I Feel: A Self-esteem Discussion Book for Kids (and Adults)*. Melbourne: Longman Cheshire.